Daddy, Where are You?

Written and illustrated by Barbara Rockaway

Daddy, where are you? I need you!

Dear Taylor,

I am your Daddy. I am here. I am all around you. Because I am with God, who is everywhere, I can also be with you. You will not see me in the same way you did before I died, but I am still here. I am with you all the time, and I promise I will never leave you.

I am writing this letter to help you know how to find me. I have always loved playing games, especially with you. Now we have a new game to play. It's like hide and seek. Come on, let's play!

Remember, I love you. First and most importantly, I love you.

I delight in you. You are my special son. I loved you before you were born, and I will love you forever. In the silence, I am always whispering, "I love you. I'm here with you."

Because I am all around you, there are many places for you to look for me. The closest is right inside.

You will find me in your heart loving you, and in your mind saying, "How ya doin'? What's up, Tay?"

You will find me every time you and Mommy kiss. You'll feel my lips with hers.

She'll feel your lips and mine together, for we will always be part of each other.

You will find me every time you get out of the water, cold and shivering.

As you wrap up in a towel, you'll feel my arms wrap around you in a big snugly hug.

You will find me in the night sky. Look to the stars and you'll see my eyes twinkling in delight of you.

Know that I'm thinking, "Buddy, you're stellar!"

You will find me every time you kneel to say your prayers. Look for me in your shadow. I'll hear your prayers and be praying with you. Remember, Buddy, "we're teammates."

You will find me when you awaken in the morning. With the songs of the birds, you'll hear me sing your name.

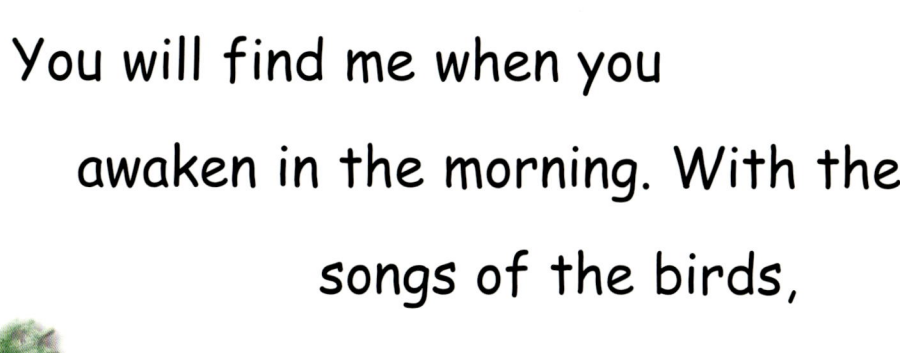

Each time you see a bluebird, know that I am happy. I'm proud of you and how you're growing.

You will find me with every white butterfly you see.

That's a sign that I am near you. At those times, you will feel me urge you to "keep moving forward."

You will find me in the touch of the breezes.

I'll tousle your hair so that you can feel my presence. And when the winds blow, I'll toss your hat for a quick game of chase.

Sometimes you will feel that no matter how hard you try, you will not be able to find me. Those will be hard times. We can't worry about that. That's when you'll need

to keep your head in the game.

We'll get through it together.

Always remember,

I will still be here, and

you will find me again.

You will find me in the ripples that form in the water after you've thrown a stone. It is then that you will see me smiling with you.

Toss the stone out as far as you can, and see how big my smile gets.

You will find me when you're fishing.
Sometimes you'll feel a tug on your line.
You'll pull up your line, and you won't find a fish.

Then you'll know I am here playing with you.
With the rippling water, I'll be laughing.

You will find me in the sky when the clouds are white and fluffy.

I'll push the clouds into pictures for you, and together we can laugh at my drawings.

You will find me when you hear the crack of the ball against your bat. That's me saying, "AWESOME! Great hit, Tay."

You will find me when you've grown older and have joined a team. Even then I will always be near. Listen for the cheers of the crowd, and know that they are my voice.

Taylor, this new game we're playing will not always be easy. It will take time and practice to see me in these new ways. But always know that I will keep playing and with practice you will get better at finding me. Remember, "it's not easy, even in practice."

Someday, to your surprise, you may discover that you've gotten good at this game. You may even learn to find me in ways I haven't mentioned. And you'll be right. I'll be there. I'll always love you, and I promise to always be with you.

Love, Daddy

Go Forward!

Timm and Taylor Snider   May 2001

Timm Wilson Snider
February 13, 1969 - June 29, 2001

As a toddler, Timm was wary of people, even those he saw frequently. Relatives visiting for holidays would often find him hiding under his crib or in his closet. However, as he matured, Timm grew not only to tolerate people, but to enjoy them. He was a natural-born leader, exuding a passion for life in general and for sports in particular. Throughout his childhood, he played baseball, basketball, hockey, soccer, golf, and raced BMX bikes. When he was older Timm ran soccer camps and clinics, mentored younger players, and became the youngest coach in the state of Wisconsin to take a girls' high school soccer team to the state tournament. Timm carried his passion for sports into his professional life, impacting the lives of co-workers and customers alike. Yet Timm's greatest passion was for his family, his wife, Sheri, and their young son, Taylor.

From the moment of Taylor's birth, Timm embraced fatherhood with all the zest and contagious enthusiasm that he had previously displayed for sports. He arranged his work schedule in order to spend two days of each week at home with Taylor. On those days, Timm and Taylor would visit relatives and friends, stroll the grounds of the zoo, throw stones in the pond by the hour, attend Brewers games, go fishing, and play at the park. They played hockey in the basement and baseball in the backyard. In the winter they went sledding and built snowmen, and in the summer they swam. By age two, Taylor could hit a pitched baseball.

Then one night the unimaginable happened. After tucking his son into bed and relaxing on the couch with his wife, Timm's heart went into an abnormal arrhythmia. He lost consciousness and died days later at age 32. His wife was three months pregnant with their second son.

Timm's personal motto was GO FORWARD!

My Uncle Timm, my Godfather, wore number 7 on many of his sports uniforms. He even signed his name with a German 7 instead of a dot over the "i". In his memory, Milwaukee Sport Club retired his soccer jersey after he died. My uncle was an awesome guy and I miss him, but I know I'll spend forever with him in Heaven, and I can't wait! Number 7 will not be forgotten.

Kyle Re, Timm's Godson

About the Author

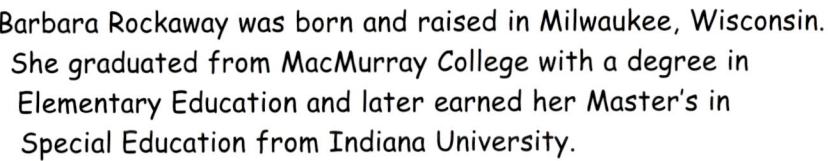

Barbara Rockaway was born and raised in Milwaukee, Wisconsin. She graduated from MacMurray College with a degree in Elementary Education and later earned her Master's in Special Education from Indiana University.

Barbara is the mother of five grown children, and has five grandchildren. Before retiring, she was an elementary school teacher for twenty years. Throughout her career, she taught preschool through 8th grade as well as Special Education classes.

During her years as a teacher, Mrs. Rockaway encountered children with unresolved grief as a result of losing a parent at a young age. When Mrs. Rockaway's nephew Timm died unexpectedly in 2001 the situation hit home and she decided to write the book, Daddy, Where Are You? to answer the questions that Timm's young son Taylor was asking.

While researching this book, Mrs. Rockaway spoke with adults who had lost a parent during their childhood. Many expressed regret about never having an opportunity to talk through their loss because family and friends became uncomfortable whenever they brought up the subject. Consequently, they just stopped talking about their experience – which resulted in unresolved grief. Using her experience relating to young children and her understanding of adult grieving, Mrs. Rockaway wrote her book with three goals in mind:
- to create a book written for children to help them understand their situation
- to provide a forum to help adults talk with children about their deceased parents in order to facilitate the discussions needed to work through the child's grief
- to create a way in which children and adults could focus in a positive way on the parent who had died.